Hidden Sins: *Hidden Iniquity*

Dr. Marlene Miles

Freshwater Press 2025

ISBN: 978-1-965772-95-9

Paperback Version

Table of Contents

HIDDEN SINS,

Hidden Iniquity

Freshwater

Hidden Sins

This book is not only about those who sin and hide it, or try to hide it, but it is also about sins that people don't even realize they either committed or have a responsibility to deal with. They don't realize that iniquity is attached to them. Until they repent, renounce, denounce and ask the Lord's forgiveness and sanctification by the Blood of Jesus, there will be iniquity to pay. Even if we pray, sometimes iniquity still plays out. David repented to God, but the first son with Bathsheba, who was conceived in **major** sin, still died because of the **iniquity**. The hidden sins may be the cause of iniquity that we don't even know is on us or in our lives.

Regarding David and Bathsheba's "love child," if we were in his little mind and life may have just been born and wondering why is this place so harsh? Why is it so uncomfortable? Why don't I feel well? I should cry, and cry, and cry, and maybe they will come and help me. I'm a baby, right? Isn't that what I should do? So as the days go on, and a week is up, it is time for that baby to leave the Earth realm, even though he just got here. *What did that baby do?*

Nothing. Nothing at all. That baby did not sin. But he inherited and paid for the iniquity of David and Bathsheba his adulterous, lying, scheming, treacherous parents. Who later became King and Queen of Israel.

The baby died. We say it hurt David; it hurt the parents, but what about the baby? The baby died because of hidden sin; the sin was hidden to the child, even though the parents both knew they had sinned. Had the iniquity played out differently, slower, the child could have suffered as a toddler, grade schooler, teen, or young adult and then the child may have fallen sick or died later. All that time, can you see how the sin would still have been hidden to the child? Which of those two parents would have ever told the child of the events surrounding his conception? Neither of them. How many sinful or very sinful parents, without the Lord's intervention would ever have the spiritual chops to understand iniquity and why horrible things have been happening to him all of his life, even though he is a prince and have a king and a queen as parents and have no need of any material thing?

It is because of the hidden sin that he inherited. How would he have ever figured that out? Most people, kids especially blame themselves or accept it and just suffer. They think that is *just the way it is.*

David and Bathsheba's baby, he had no way to speak and pray and beg forgiveness from God; he had no way of even knowing what was going on.

This kind of hidden sin, folks. When a person, saved or unsaved, spiritually savvy, or not, gets blindsided and suffers loss, constant or chronic disappointment or devastation because of sin that overtakes him or her.

What Are Hidden Sins?

You have set our iniquities before you, our
secret sins in the light of your presence.
(Psalm 90:8)

Our sins, even those hidden from
others, are fully known to God. Our secret
sins should not be protected; they should be
confessed. However, I am not talking about
sins we commit and then try to hide or cover
up *as if.* Just because no other human knows
about them, or one other human and you've
both sworn to secrecy doesn't make them any
less sins. David and Bathsheba knew they
had sinned. David even confessed and
received forgiveness from the Lord, but there
was still iniquity to pay.

Whoever conceals his transgressions will
not prosper, but he who confesses and

forsakes them will obtain mercy. (Proverbs 28:13)

For nothing is hidden that will not be made manifest, nor is anything secret that will not be known and come to light. (Luke 8:17)

Who can discern his errors? Declare me innocent from hidden faults. (Psalm 19:12)

All the ways of a man are clean in his own eyes, they are pure in that man's eyes. The person who is quick to judge and accuses others usually thinks himself pure and perfect.

When you realize that you are human, just as they are, and consider the struggles you have in your own humanity, you can be gracious, kind, tolerant, and patient with others. Not to the point of enabling, but to the point of showing them Christ and *watering* so God can give the increase.

It is either hard to see or admit to one's own errors and hidden faults. We must seek God, repent, and ask forgiveness and deliverance from sins we may not even be aware of.

If we all have sinned and fallen short of the Glory of God, and we need tender mercies every morning. WHAT **DID WE DO YESTERDAY**? WHAT DID WE DO LAST NIGHT? WHY DO WE NEED MERCY IN THE MORNING, JUST AS THE DAY IS BREAKING OR THE SUN IS SHINING OR BEFORE WE EVEN GET OUT OF BED?

David and Bathsheba's firstborn needed Mercy, and he too, just got here, and would have no knowledge or recall of what he may have done to even need Mercy.

Did I do that? Steve Urkel

King David lusts, (2 Samuel 11-12) and that's a sin common to man. in the case of king David, and in the case of sin, you can only try to hide a sin with more sin—, by committing more sin

Saints of God, when you try to cover sin, you are covering the evil work of devils and demons, even the devil himself. WHY? Why would you do that? You can't, but why would you try? You can't, you only compromise yourself further. So, don't do that.

Sin must be confessed, not hidden.

Or, you can confess sin and by repentance the sin can be forgiven and atoned for, by the Blood of Jesus, but hiding it from God, is impossible. In Genesis, God asked, Adam, where are you? He was looking for them because they tried to hide. God found them and put them out of the Garden. Cain tried to hide his sin. God found Cain. Sin cannot be hidden from God.

This book isn't even about sins that are sins that you didn't know they were sins so you may want to plead ignorance – no. Ignorance is no defense. This book is not just about secret sins, although that is too prevalent. Sin creates sin cycles that people get trapped in and need to be broken out of.

Sin is anointed; it is anointed by the devil. People like sin, at least at first, and that is often why they do it. But then the sin cycle begins.

I'm accusing no one. Sin can be forced on a person, and that we know all too well.

The only way to break free of a sin is by a power greater than the power that invited you + courted you + empowered you to sin in the first place.

So, finally, what kind of sin is this book really about? It is about **hidden sin,** and in answering Steve Urkel – no, you may not have done that. It is about sins that stalk you. Transgressions that seem to overtake you, Iniquity finds you. Because of hidden sins and hidden iniquity, people are paying for things they didn't buy. It is about markers in your blood that compel you.

This book is about sins that you didn't commit, but they are accounted to you. The iniquity of those sins has been imparted and imputed to you. This is where people are paying for things they didn't *buy;* it's because of their blood.

Ancestral sins, the sins of our parents and our ancestors, the sins that they didn't

12

repent for, the sins they may have tried to hide, or maybe they didn't even try to hide them. We don't know if our ancestors were outright sinners or not. We hope not. We want to believe they weren't blatant sinners, but I ask the question: when you've done all you know to do, when you have been saved, repented for everything you know that you did, that you can repent for, you have sought deliverance full force, but there seems to still be iniquity coming at you—WHY?

Have you asked God, WHY?

You may have done spiritual mapping in your family, all the way up and down your family tree. You may have mapped your neighborhood, your community, even your city you live in and you've repented for everything that you've found to repent for.

There are sins that are hidden to you, maybe you've collected them unawares along the way, or they have found you because of your blood. The iniquity that looks for everyone in your bloodline.

1. Lord, reveal to me all my hidden sins, every one of them, in the Name of Jesus.
2. Not just my secret sins, but also things I do, and I am not aware that they are sins. Lord, reveal to me sins that are hidden that I don't even know I'm responsible for or that there is **iniquity** following me because of ancient sins and ancient altars, in the Name of Jesus.

Generational iniquity is because of the sin of ancestors, perhaps it is slated that everyone in the next generation or the one after that will have to deal with thus and so, and you happen to be that generation of your bloodline.

Collective Captivity (familial, group, or territorial curses are present when what's happening to you is happening to everyone in your family, unless you serve their idol *gods*, so now it is trying to oppress you. The idol gods will come to you to punish you because you are not serving them--, because you are saved, you serve only Christ Jesus.

Saints of God, don't get saved if you don't mean it. Backsliding, and taking your hands off the plow is very dangerous (Luke 9:62). Don't get deliverance if you are not planning to as Jesus told people over and again: go and sin no more.

When Jesus had lifted up himself, and saw none but the woman, he said unto her, Woman, where are those thine accusers? hath no man condemned thee?

She said, No man, Lord. And Jesus said unto her, Neither do I condemn thee: go, and sin no more. (John 8:10-11)

If you've accepted salvation and profess Christ, then you've got to at least try to be saved, walk saved, or the condition of that man will be worse than it was before he got delivered. You can't just run to the LORD for deliverance because you can't take the oppression anymore, knowing fully you want relief so you can go back to your free-spirit, party lifestyle.

Big Mistake. God is not mocked.

When the unclean spirit is gone out of a man, he walketh through dry places, seeking rest, and findeth none. Then he saith, I will return into my house from whence I came out; and when he is come, he findeth *it* empty, swept, and garnished. **Then goeth he, and taketh with himself seven other spirits more wicked than himself, and they enter in and dwell there: and the last *state* of that man is worse than the first. Even so shall it be also unto this wicked generation.** (Matthew 12:43-45)

Down low sins could be sins you didn't even know were sins. Sins your parents didn't know were sins, sins your ancestors didn't know were sins...

Sins that are sins, but everyone is doing it so you think it is okay. It is not. Unforgiveness, anger, all works of the flesh have iniquity with them. Maybe you're a good-hearted person and you don't do any of that, but did your parents keep grudges against people? Did your ancestors keep feuds going? Even family feuds?

You don't know. So pray and repent. Repent down your bloodline all the way back to Adam and Eve and ask the Lord to remove the iniquity in your bloodline, in the Name of Jesus.

3. Lord, reveal to me all my hidden sins, every one of them, every hidden sin that is the cause of stubborn problems in my life, in the Name of Jesus.

Yeah, that –, but also defilements that come from devils and demons, especially in the dream

> What? know ye not that he which is joined to an harlot is one body? for two, saith he, shall be one flesh. (1 Corinthians 6:16)

That means that if you've had *relations* with a harlot, a *player*, a whatever you call someone for the streets, then you have **joined in their sin with them and you share in their iniquity.** Not just their sin for the moment that you are committing with them, but the collective aggregate of their sins and iniquity that they have not repented of. Add to that the iniquity they were born with. Who among us was born with a clean slate?

> Behold, I was shapen in iniquity; and in sin did my mother conceive me. (Psalm 51:5)

Ladies, you like the bad boys? What kind of demons does a bad boy have that makes him *bad*? When you like a bad boy, you are liking the false front that he is displaying to make up for the fact that he is demonized, oppressed and anything else that he is trying to hide. You like a façade. You like false bravado. You like *fake*?

I can say that because what is "bad" in a bad boy is not his submission to God, it is rebellion. Rebellion is sin and it comes with transgression, and iniquity.

If you could see the real demons he's wrestling with--, if you could see your own, you'd repent right now. But, seriously, if you could see his, you would run in the opposite direction, not cozy up to them.

Something could be a *hidden sin* because you don't think that you did anything wrong, after all, everyone else is doing it. Maybe it was one time, one mistake --- well, you've become **one** with them, 1 Corinthians 6:16.

You don't know who else has become *one* with them before you, and except by prayer and the Holy Spirit will you know what demons the last person they were with had. You don't know how many demons a person brought you in that act.

Even if this person professes Christ, but especially if they don't–, what have you brought into your life?

Did I do that? No, you didn't but if you did the deed with the person who did, then you did. You are guilty by association.

You also need to break every soul tie with that person, each and every soul tie, with each and every person; call them by name in your prayers. Then file for a spiritual divorce from them, each and every one of them. go to the Courts of Heaven.

If you have any items they gave you; any points of contact, get rid of it all, burn it.

When It Was Forced on You

Defilement has iniquity with it.

Did I do that? No, you didn't even do anything, did you? If you are defiled, most often, but not always, it is not consensual, but it could be. If you are defiled in the night, in the sleep, in the dream, then it makes sense that you will need tender mercies in the morning. The morning after is a whole lot more than a walk of shame, although there will be shame--, or there should be, unless the sinner is reprobate.

If that *thing* had relations with you, even without your consent, does that mean that you *joined* with it? If you didn't then how did you get defiled? It wanted to defile you to block your future blessings. It wanted to defile you to keep you in lockdown, in captivity. It wanted to defile you to steal from you.

It probably wanted to join with you because GOD loves you and you can be redeemed and enter into the presence of the LORD; -- it can't.

But mostly it wanted to defile you because it is on assignment. Demons take their assignments seriously or there will be hell to pay. Literally.

What are you doing about it?

Spirit spouse can be the defiler in the spirit, in the dream. Is a *spirit spouse* a harlot?

Yes.

How much of a harlot? What's the *body count* of a demon? What is the body count of a defiling demon?

Every time you have had illegal sex, which is any sex that is not with your covenanted marriage partner, to include solo sex, there was at least one demon present, and **involved--, participating.**

How many times? Don't tell me, tell the Lord, and repent.

What is the *body count* of an astral projecting stalker and defiler? Only the Holy Spirit will tell you the truth if you ask that question. Pray against evil human persecutors and against astral projecting *humans*. There is a section on Command the Month of March prayers about this on the Dr. Marlene Miles You Tube channel. https://www.youtube.com/@drmiles8271

You can ask any person you are intimate with about their *body count*, and they *may* tell you the truth, they may not. They may be proud of it and brag to you. but, saints of God, you won't know the body count of *all the people the defiling person or entity has been with.*

What is the body count of a person who is so pleased and proud to go into the night and attack, or rape men and or women because they *can*? Do you think they only did it once? Do you think you're the only one? of course, not!

People, astral sex is sex with demons, it is disgusting, and it transfers spiritual iniquity and physical disease to humans.

Illegal sex and dream sex, which is also illegal, defiles the human. If you don't realize it, do anything about it, or know that you can do something about it... or how to do something about it, you will stay defiled. Defiled means unclean, biblically.

The unclean had to sit outside the gate and if you read in the Bible, it was until the next day. So they were exiled outside of the city, outside the gate and were considered unclean until evening, or 6pm, which is the next day. *Outside the gate* means out of the presence of God, couldn't worship, couldn't sacrifice, couldn't hang out with friends and family. You were in no-man's land because of being unclean or defiled.

If you lose a spiritual day, how much time, how much progress have you lost? In terms of money, I heard that the US economy would lose about 2.5 billion dollars on the day after Super Bowl because of all the people who would not come to work that day. How much money do you lose if you miss a day from work? How many perks might you lose? How much progress? Will you have to start all over again? That's what the devil is hoping the reason he sends a demon to defile you.

You may get attacked in the night and you get put in timeout, but you are not the instigator, but you become one with that defiled--, *thing*.

Think of playing a board game, you're making progress then somebody gets the ability to knock you off the board and you lose all your progress and have to go back to the starting position again.

Do all you know to protect your relationship with God and your progress in life. Stay. Prayed. Up.

Once defiled, you are very defilable--- again and again. That makes you trash, a dumpster in the spirit. If you are marked by that *spirit spouse*, other demons passing by will see that mark and say, *Oh, I can go there.*
4. Lord, forbid, in Jesus' Name.

There is no way any of us can look down on Rahab, or Mary Magdalene, or the woman with the alabaster box because any of us, **males and females**, could be prostitutes in the spirit and not even know it. Folks, you'd better pray and don't go to bed unless you are prayed up.

If you are unsaved or a dry Christian, regarding astral sex, anyone could be having sex with any witch, even a relative and you get defiled because they already are defiled by virtue of being a witch. Defiled people defile people. Defiled things defile people.

Astral sex defiles and brings on hidden sin. Yes, the sex is hidden, because it may be wiped from your dream or the memory. It is heinous and shameful; you might not want to tell anyone. But tell it to Jesus. Repent, even though you're the victim. If you don't repent you will be the victim over and over.

Ask the Holy Spirit to tell you or show you, else, you're going to be in a vicious, evil cycle. This is a *spirit spouse*, but it is a human spirit that is astral projecting to victimize you.

If you have been attacked in the night by an astral rapist, consider that they are the worst of the worst. They have probably committed every possible sin and are probably reprobate.

5. Let every astral projecting spirit spouse DIE, in the Name of Jesus.

(More on this in my book, **Astral Projected Spirit Spouse, DIE!** https://a.co/d/fpcYgyA

What You Worship You *Join* With

What else was that person you were dealing with, into?

Did they have skull tattoos and all kinds of satanic jewelry? Were they a satanist? Or did they just *look like* one, dress like one, and wear tattoos like a satanist?

Then they became a satanist; it is **their** hidden sin—it is hidden to them if they don't realize they did it. By putting on their stuff and taking their marks, you become one of them. If they don't know they did it, it is a sin that is hidden to them. There may have been demonic suggestions for days, weeks, months, or even years, but eventually they did it. They did it to themselves.

"Ye worship ye know not what: we know what we worship: for salvation is of the Jews." (John 4:22A)

Folks, non-spiritual people who know nothing of God, of the Bible, or spirituality, of sin are some of the most dangerous people in the world. They could cluelessly bring anything to you. You like them, you trust them, you love them? Then you have stopped vetting them and they now have free reign in your life. They could be doing anything while they are not with you and bringing you anything, on the regular.

So, this last person you dealt with, or anyone that you dealt with--, did they practice witchcraft? Do you absolutely know that they didn't? Did you *join* with them and become one with that? Not by practicing dark arts, but by being *united* with them by association? *Spirits* transfer, you know. Did you by chance become *one* with them in the sex act? *Spirits* readily transfer during sex. Even once.

So, you see now that you may have a lot more repenting to do than you thought.

What secret things did your parents and ancestors do?

You don't know. You could be paying for stuff they've done, so be very comprehensive in your repentance prayers. Be sure to renounce and denounce every sin, yes to free yourself, but so you don't, through your own blood, pass this iniquity down to your children, and their children.

A person could be having sex in the dream or eating in the dream; both are defilement. They could be having other kinds of evil initiations--, if they don't remember their dreams or if their dreams are wiped. The iniquity from hidden sins could be holding them back, blocking their successes in life and in business. Hidden sins could be the cause of stubborn health issues that don't clear up.

Joy ride? Dream sex is not free sex, it is not a joy ride. Dream sex is like a criminal coming to pick you up in a stolen car for a "joy ride." The one who stole the car, the criminal gets arrested and so does the person who was in the car on the joy ride, even though they didn't steal the car.

Repent of anything that you may have done that may have allowed a hidden sin and its iniquity to come into your life.

6. Every hidden curse that was placed on me in the womb, die, in the Name of Jesus.
7. Every hidden curse that was placed upon my life when I was a baby, die, in the Name of Jesus.
8. Every hidden curse that I inherited from my parents, or through the iniquity of my ancestors, receive Holy Ghost Fire and die, in the Name of Jesus.
9. Every curse of spiritual marriage that is in my life, burn to ashes, in the Name of Jesus.
10. Every covenant allowing the curse of *spirit spouse* in my life, break by the power in the Blood of Jesus.
11. Holy Ghost Fire, burn every hidden curse in my life to ashes, in the Name of Jesus.

12. Any hidden curse that is placed on me in the dream, in the night, in the sleep, die, in the Name of Jesus.

13. I reject, break and curse every evil initiation in the sleep, in the dream, in the Name of Jesus.

- Lord, reveal to me all my hidden sins, every one of them, in the Name of Jesus.

14. Holy Spirit, show me how to pray against hidden sins, in the Name of Jesus.

15. Lord, I break free and loose my destiny from destruction caused by hidden curses, in the Name of Jesus.

16. Any obstacle, barrier, roadblock or wall that is stopping me from forward progress, crumble to pieces, fall down and become dust, in the Name of Jesus.

17. Every witchcraft curse that is attacking me from the dark, be exposed and die, in the Name of Jesus.

18. Every hidden curse and every hidden sin is defeated, in the Name of Jesus. My health, become robust and spring forth, in the Name of Jesus.

19. Thank You, Lord, for hearing and answering prayers, in the Name of Jesus.
20. As a worship, pray Psalm 9.

King's Honor

It is the glory of God to conceal a thing, but
the honor of a king, is to search out a
matter. (Proverbs 25:2)

Glory here means *kabod*, which is
really the weight of glory or the splendor, the
gloriousness of it. It is glorious to search out
matters.

It is kingly to search out a matter.
Jesus, for example spoke in parables because
everything was not for everyone. Some of
those Parables we are still searching out and
getting revelation today, from glory to glory.
God likes for us to search out things, it is why
we have the Holy Spirit who is the Spirit of
Understanding. It is why those who don't
have the Holy Spirit interpret the bible
literally. One must have the Holy Spirit to
understand God.

Can you imagine that if you had the same spirit as your spouse how well the two of you could get along? If you had the same spirit as your coworkers, or your friends and family there would be no skiffs and no divisions among you. Can you imagine how productive every aspect of your life would be?

Well, it they have the Holy Spirit, and you have the Holy Spirit, things can be glorious.

So, God likes for us to look for and find out things that are unknown. Mysterious maybe, but things that we need to know about.

God hides some things on purpose, because everything is not for everyone, and everything is not for everyone in the *same season*. So, most of the time we will search out things when we're **ready** for it so it doesn't confuse us.

Hidden Stuff

And the devil? Surely, he will hide or try to hide things from mankind. Yeah, things like evil contracts and things he's stolen from us. Fine print in evil contracts and as I like to say, fine-fine print in evil covenants.

From Genesis we learned that the serpent was more subtle. He was very subtle, very sneaky.

So, we've been taught to forgive others when they're taking things from us, such as our coats and our cloak. Things we learn to share, give or do without, might be our jacket or favorite pencil. And that's all stuff that we can **see**.

What about the things we can't see, the things that are hidden to us, hidden from us? We may not even know what's happening with those things. What have we been taught about that? So, as I said, perhaps God has hidden things for our protection or for the protection of the things.

Or maybe some things have been hidden by the enemy of our souls. Perhaps he is hiding the **real** stuff that he's doing against us while we quibble over coats and cloaks and our favorite pencil in the natural.

We count cloaks and personal effects that maybe a thief or a robber might want to steal from us that are still under our stewardship. Therefore, we are responsible for those things. But could it all just be a smoke screen while the devil hides the real stuff that he's really trying to do against us?

Steal, kill and destroy. Steal destinies. Kill hope. Destroy joy. Steal peace, kill careers, destroy health, marriages, families, lives.

Christians, we were taught in school to do unto others. Going about doing good deeds, we should do good, and forgive those who don't. We also need to consider the unseen things that may be happening to us that might be right under our radar. Without spiritual eyes we won't have a clue. Without discernment or ears to hear God, we won't know what's happening spiritually and we may focus only on the natural.

How does losing your coat, your cloak and your favorite pencil make you **feel**? Not emotionally, but how do you feel spiritually? What do you discern about the situation now that you no longer have what has been taken from you?

Now, what you *discern* is really what you've lost, not the pencil.

Not only that, if you allow your coat, cloak and pencil to leave your stewardship, will God ask you about them? Will you have to give account if it was someone else's, and you were just watching it for them? Does it open the door where the devil now says, I got the coat, cloak, and pencil, now what else can I take?

The Senses

Touch is one of the five senses, so is vision. What's all the focus on hidden things? Hidden things are things we cannot see. So, consider that what is happening in the natural may be happening because we missed something in the spiritual that would have stopped or prevented the thing in the natural from happening to us.

If we can see spiritually, things will not be hidden in the spirit. Through the eyes of faith, through spiritual eyes, we can be made to know and see what's happening in the spirit. When it is in the spirit, it is **before** it gets to the natural world. When it gets to the natural, that's when it's going to impact flesh. Sometimes when things impact our flesh, it's harder to deal with. If we could just deal with it in the spirit, it would make prevention is worth a pound of cure, a true adage. When something is happening in the flesh we feel it. When it happens in the spirit, we must see it spiritually, hear it spiritually, or **know** it. **Knowing** is higher than touch, higher than *feeling*. Feeling and touch are of the physical and the flesh. Spiritual vision is by the spirit. Spirit is always higher than soul and higher than flesh.

Am I posing that every natural attack is the result of something that we've missed in the Spirit? The person who is tossed about in the natural from day to day and moment to moment is most likely spiritually weak and doesn't know anything spiritually. That person is probably not praying and missing what is coming down the pike in the spirit and not doing anything about it ahead of time.

This person can be easily jumped into a demonic timeline, into survival mode, by the devil because of their own lack of discipline and spiritual faith and growth. You are responsible spiritually for where you should be in the spirit based on when you got saved. Folks, small demons are dealing with the person who is still the spiritual child that he came into the Kingdom as when he got saved. He is a plaything, a ball of yarn to evil demonic kittens. That's not you, right?

God does not want us, ignorant.

So, you had a dream the other night. If you do nothing concerning that dream, because of not knowing that what was seen in the dream was a problem, that's now your problem. We thought it was fun. We may agree with it.

Sex in the dream, maybe. Maybe we don't know what to do with it, or maybe we're just too lazy to do anything about it. If we don't do anything about something that is negative, in a dream, for instance, a covenant is formed because we agree with it and **we agreed with it by not disagreeing with it**. Dream life is spirit life.

Now that he's made a covenant with you, by your own silence, the enemy can bring his program and disaster from the **spirit**, to the natural. How long will it take to get from the spirit to the natural? It depends on a lot of things. It could take years; it could take only hours.

So, something is or remains mysterious or hidden to us because we don't believe it, or we don't want to believe it. We didn't see it. We don't believe what we saw, or it was really hidden to our spiritual eyes--, if we even have spiritual vision. Spiritual vision and hearing are closed by sin, folks.

If we don't have spiritual eyes, what's hidden to our belief system, is hidden to our minds. We learn that in the practice of medicine a doctor can only *see* what he knows when he is diagnosing and treating.

We don't believe it because we don't believe. Our belief system doesn't allow us to even believe this. You could see something and say, God, I can't even believe my eyes. You may not be able to wrap your head around it because you just don't think like that. Well then, this *something* will stay hidden, if you can't or won't believe it.

Many don't believe that witches are real. Therefore, they won't believe that witchcraft is real and therefore they cannot see the signs and symptoms of curses, even if they are on them.

Maybe people don't want spiritual eyes because seeing by the spirit is not popular in the circles you travel in. Maybe it's not cool, or you don't want people to see you as weird.

Without spiritual eyes or without spiritual eyesight or vision, night dreams can easily be mistaken and taken literally when they need to be interpreted spiritually. Without spiritual vision, where God is showing us something important, we may take it as nothing, or as a fluke or, as, , entertainment, or a pork chop dream.

A woman had a fight with her husband because of something she dreamed that she took **literally**. Maybe she shouldn't have. Or maybe she should have. We need spiritual vision to know what any dream really means. Else, a meaning or the purpose of it, the cause of it, will escape the dreamer.

So, without spiritual vision, we may get or do the opposite of what God intended.

How can we walk progressively? How can we walk forward in our lives? If our path is hidden, we wouldn't know where to walk. How can we still have successes? Only if we can see to know where to step, and or hear the Lord who will tell us.

Be a lamp unto my feet, and a light unto my path (Psalm 119:`05)

So, if you cannot see spiritually, then there's gonna be failures in life instead of success. If the path is hidden if we can't see things clearly without spiritual eyes. Maybe we end up in bondage instead of in liberty and freedom. Maybe we end up in hardship and problems instead of ease and solutions. Maybe we end up walking in fear instead of faith because we can't see the path we're supposed to be on.

21. In the Name of Jesus. I pray that our spiritual eyes will be opened. Amen.

Is Your Circle *Cool*?

It may not be popular in the circles where you travel to see spiritually, or maybe just not popular to talk about it. Maybe you should just not talk about it because we need Wisdom to know how to conduct ourselves in whatever circles we travel.

Sometimes the Lord may tell us to be quiet. He'll tell us something, but tell us to be quiet about it. It is not time to share it--, yet, or ever.

If you can't connect with the people in your circle, do you all share the *same* Spirit? Well, maybe the Lord wants you to change the circles that you travel in. Although this takes Wisdom, you've gotta ask God.

Most often, I believe that before I say something that I know or something that I believe is spiritually sensitive, I'll ask the Holy Spirit, Can I share this? And Holy Spirit will give you release, or say, either "*Yes*," or "*No*," quickly within you, that you must not share that. So, it's OK to have spiritual eyes, even if everybody else in your group doesn't. Maybe you are the person who's supposed to have spiritual eyes for your group or your family, your friends, or in your workplace. Amen.

Spiritual Eyes

With spiritual eyes, if we're around people who are carnal, who don't have spiritual vision, then a lot of those people may think we're nuts if we tell them what we really saw, what we think we saw, what we heard in the spirit, because some things are still hidden to a lot of people. If you're one of the elect who God allows to see and hear, then praise God.

Because we must search out some matters. Some things are hidden from us to protect us, some things are hidden to protect those things. And some things are hidden because there's an enemy to our soul, to our lives.

With spiritual eyes we can see and know.

Invisibility

It could be the wish of many children at some time in their childhood to be a superhero or be invisible. Criminals want this superpower so they can get away with crimes such as stealing. As long as you don't believe in devils and demons and refuse to see them, they remain more powerful by being invisible.

We learn from Genesis that the serpent in the Garden was more subtle. Too many may not be able to guess what the devil is gonna do next. But maybe we can. OK, he's gonna steal, kill and destroy. But how? That's spiritually discerned, isn't it? It's spiritually seen. It's spiritually heard. It's spiritually felt, it may have to be *discerned*. The devil is invisible, he doesn't sleep.

So just because you don't think that other humans can become invisible or that is not a thing, doesn't mean that it's not a thing. Just because your belief system doesn't allow you to believe it right now, doesn't mean that it doesn't happen or couldn't happen.

You should ask God about matters that you need to search out so you can learn about spiritual things to be looked into.

Maybe all this stuff is just too scary to think about. And you don't wanna think about it, know about it, or look into it. We need to grow up, in the Name of Jesus.

How many of us have entertained angels, unaware? Were they *invisible*? Maybe, or maybe they took human form.

Have you seen something or seen a person and they're suddenly gone? How many times have you seen people that don't really look completely human, like there's something off about them. How many times have you seen a thing, but no one else can see what you are looking right at? Some things have been hidden from us for our protection. How many times have you been with somebody? They pointed out something to you that they saw, but you completely missed it? You didn't see anything what they saw, or vice versa.

Viruses and bacteria are invisible, but they still exist and can do a lot of harm. There's a lot of invisible stuff in this world. The unseen world is what drives what we see in our natural world; therefore, we need spiritual eyes.

22. Lord, grant spiritual eyes, spiritual vision, in the Name of Jesus.

Jesus saith unto him, Thomas, because thou hast seen me, thou hast believed: blessed are they that have not seen, and yet have believed. (John 20:29)

What does that even mean? The Bible talks about angels and devils and demons and spiritual wickedness. And then there's God and there's Jesus Do we see them in the natural No. They're spiritually, "seen", discerned, heard. In a sense, they're hidden.

Spiritual things are foolishness to the carnal man; those things are hidden from that carnal man's mindset. His belief system will not *allow* him to see things that a spiritual person may see with their spiritual eyes.

Jesus spoke in parables because what He was teaching wasn't for everybody. Some He called evil, and others were vipers. If God assigned you to teach some people but you knew some evil and some vipers were among them, would you teach anyway? Yes, you would, if God told you to. But using Wisdom, Jesus found a way to do that so that by the Spirit the saved folks would understand and those who were unsaved and literal wouldn't know what He was talking about. Some of that stuff was *hidden* to be revealed another day.

God loves to reveal Himself to us—when we are ready. There are some things that are hidden in plain sight. We have to search it out.

Don't you try to hide things from your kids by spelling words that they don't know, or you *think* they don't know how to S-P-E-L-L? You use those words right in front of them but they do not know what you are talking about. Keep sending them to school; they will learn how to S-P-E-L-L.

Saints, this could be also why faith comes by hearing and not by seeing, because without faith it's impossible to please God. Lord knows, we may not have spiritual ears, but we should be able to hear the voice of the Good Shepherd.

There are altars that are speaking over our lives and into our lives and the sound is so low. There are spiritual altars in the spirit. We can't see them, but they are impacting our lives; they are hidden. Or maybe we have chosen not to hear, or we've chosen not to see.

There are cell phone ringtones that if you're under 30, you can't hear. Would you really want to? Is that important to your life? Does it impact your life? Probably not. But we really do need to be hearing spiritual things, and discerning when it is God and when it is not God. We need to be seeing those things. We need to know the Lord is speaking to us as He speaks to our heart. As long as we can hear God, we shouldn't care that much about cell phone towers, should we? Via cellphones we only hear from other humans, not God.

Hidden Altars

Let's say, regarding this hidden altar, you go to friends or families houses and they got a whole altar set up. Do you know it? Not necessarily because an altar can look like anything, could look like nothing. It could look like decor. It could look like something weird. You may think it's some kind of an art installation, not realizing it's an altar.

They could have an altar in a private part of their home that you are not privy to. Either way, what's on that altar is a clue to who they are worshipping, what they're doing in the spirit, who they're serving, and who they believe is helping them, giving them things, or protecting them.

Do you know what they are using that altar to do? You won't unless they tell you or the Holy Spirit reveals it to you.

What happens in an altar impacts your life. What happens at an altar is worship, and it is the invoking of *spirits* or a *spirit*. Hopefully it's God, but unfortunately not always. A *spirit* comes to that altar, it may be directed to bring evil into your life, or if that Spirit is God, it will bless your life.

If it's against God, it's evil. And once this altar gets started, it doesn't stop, until a power greater than that altar tears it down, breaks it up--, stops it. Else, it goes into the generations. It goes forever until a spiritual person with discernment, with spiritual vision, with knowledge, with Wisdom, with authority, breaks that altar up, at least spiritually, because it is not always possible to break up a natural altar.

Breaking up an altar means breaking up or reversing the results of that altar over someone's life, or in the lives of their family, or their generations. A minister, for instance, breaks up an altar when he's ministering deliverance for a believer. Amen. Breaking up an altar is deliverance.

Just because something is spiritual doesn't mean it's God. Evil altars are spiritual. Curses are spiritual, but they are not of God. Curses are the results of evil covenants from evil altars. Demons are sent to enforce a curse.

What mom or dad is gonna tell their children about all the stuff they did when they were young, or stuff that their parents did that they may or may not even know about? Whose going to tell about the things that they hid from their own parents?

Worse, they may not have a clue because it is hidden from them, as well.

That's how evil covenants last into lifetimes and through bloodlines, bringing evil into your life. Out of sight out of mind? No, it doesn't work like that. Whether you see it or not, if an evil altar is emanating against you, then it just is.

An evil altar could have been established against your bloodline, anywhere in the world, generations ago and evil from that altar could still be happening to your bloodline, and maybe it has reached you by now. You need spiritual eyes. I need spiritual eyes. We need to see in the spirit. We need to hear in the spirit. We are spiritual beings who need to know what to do, and we need to do something about this evil altar; even if you're saying, there's still nothing to do.

Let's say years ago, your parents did something. They may not have known what they did. They could have offended a witch and never known it; witches are easy to offend. They may have had a curse issued against them and may have never known it. The curse may not have been on them, it could have been on their generations. They didn't know there was a curse and certainly not what the curse is. You have to learn the Bible, what the curses are for various sins, and maybe just as a prayer warrior, hit all of them. You don't even know what *spirit* is dishing out what against you. You just know your life is uncomfortable. It's not just going to go away on its own. You have to make it go away. You have to make it expire against you and your bloodline.

Hidden Spirit Spouse

Why would I have to learn that there are over 30 different kinds of *spirit spouses* this week? Oh, I know--, so I can tell you. **There are over 30 different kinds of *spirit spouses*.**

I also had to learn that so I could pray against all of these different kinds of *spirit spouses*.

Sometimes, you don't even know a *spirit spouse* is there. Some evil somebody could have sent a *spirit spouse* to you. *Spirit spouses* stay in families for generation after generation. It could be emanating from evil foundation. It could emanate from an evil altar. Could be something you attracted. Hidden *spirit spouse*. You don't even know it's there because it's not trying to get physical with you like the other ones. Maybe it's just there to ruin your life, maybe just to steal. But that is no reason not to be kingly and search it out and get rid of it.

Spirit spouses block their victims from getting married. Are you a person who's been wanting to get married and you're not? You don't understand why. Could be *spirit spouse*. Could be *hidden spirit spouse*. *Spirit spouses* cause barrenness and impotence. *Spirit spouses* chase off suitors. You could be dating and sinning up a storm and nothing bad seems to happen. But as soon as you show interest in getting married, male or female, *spirit spouse* may rear its evil demonic head. *Spirit spouses* cause people to be rejected, often suddenly, and for no apparent reason.

Spirit spouses jack up finances; they are there to steal. They cause sickness. They cause divorces. *Spirit spouses* cause confusion and unnecessary arguments in the home or in marriages. Yeah, a married person can have a *spirit spouse*. Both parties in a marriage can have *spirit spouses.* One person can have multiple *spirit spouses.*

Spirit spouse can cause sudden hatred by your own spouse. Do you remember when you were sinning up a storm a couple of paragraphs back? Do you recall that you thought you were okay? You thought nothing was happening? That could be where *spirit spouse* came from--, the iniquity from your own sin, (usually sexual sin). You invited it by illegal sex. Like a stray cat, it doesn't want to leave, and it wants you to itself.

It is defiling and destructive and you have to get rid of it so you can not only get married, but live happily married and be successful in life.

Hidden Defilement

Eating in the dream is a form of defilement. Getting busy on a date with somebody that you are not married to is defilement.

Getting busy on a date in the dream is defilement. It is? Yes, it is. Eating and drinking in the dream is also defilement. Initiated into a coven, even in a dream, and against your knowledge is defilement. Doing anything that God says don't do, or anything against the Word, or the Will of God is defilement.

This could all be **hidden** to you because it is often done in the night, and dreams can be blanketed or wiped. Not only that, but demons also come in masquerade, and you may think you are having sex in the dream with your real spouse.

There is no reason to have sex in the dream with your real spouse; your real spouse is right there with you (usually). That dream sex was with a demon with your spouse's face.

If you are initiated into any evil in the dream, you may not know about that either, but you are interested in different things, suddenly. You start dressing in black all the time. Witchy things attract you and you are not even aware that they are witchy, you just know that you like them. You have been defiled and maybe get defiled every night or regularly and may not have a clue of it.

This is a hidden sin. You could be a blind witch because of dream initiation; that is hidden sin. It's happening, but you don't know a thing about it.

These activities form hidden contracts with the devil that open doors for evil to enter a life. So, if the enemy could do something to you in the natural, it is because of something that previously happened in the spiritual realm.

For example, in a dream you thought, oh wow, I'm really *pulling*, this guy is good looking, or this dream girl is really hot. So, within that dream, you just went along with sex in the dream. But that was violence against you; that is spiritual violence.

The kingdom of Heaven suffers violence, and the violent take it by force. (Matthew 11:12)

Saints of God, I am not accusing you of anything. You could get caught up in sex in the dream and not be able to stop it. It could be so fast, or you are totally asleep or sleep paralyzed. You fight dream sex when you are awake, building up your spirit man to defend you against such when you are asleep. I am not saying you are doing it on purpose or enjoying it. Personally, I ask the Holy Spirit to wake me up if any type of dream attack is about to happen so I can pray about it immediately.

As well, be sure to cancel every demonic dream.

We Should Be Hidden

When it comes to what should be hidden; **we** should be hidden. Our lives should be hidden and protected from all this spiritual violence. However, if we are to come out fighting, then Lord, let us fight and win! We should be hidden in Christ. We should be hidden under the shadow of the most High God, under His wings. We should be hidden in the cleft of the Rock; hidden in Christ.

Christ is a whole realm, and we should be in it. Because we serve a God who hides His servants. And while we are hidden in God, He works on us. He perfects us. He teaches us. He breaks us sometimes and puts us back together. He purifies us, He refines us, He anoints us. Hallelujah. So, we come out with a greater anointing and a greater power, and we can do greater works in the Earth. Because Jesus said, **I go to the Father**.

This morning, in a dream, I was standing in a pulpit, telling the congregation that the Lord says there's a storm coming and we all need to go to higher ground. Some storms are hidden. Sometimes we can look outside and see the wind blowing and the sky darkening, we may even see drops of rain pouring sideways from the sky, with hail, thunder, and lightning.

But some storms are not natural, some are emotional, some are financial. Some relational. Many storms are hidden. In the dream I was telling the people in the congregation, there is a storm coming. The Lord says there's a storm coming. And we need to go to higher ground.

The devil has hidden plans against us, even storms planned against us? We can pray and ask God to reveal those things to us. Pray and practice Godly discipline, so that God will take us to higher ground. He'll take us higher. He'll take us to the Rock that is higher than we are. He'll take us to safety. We can see those storms if we have spiritual eyes. All the secret things belong to God. He will shine Light on them, and they will be revealed, in due season. Hallelujah. Nothing in all creation is hidden from God's sight. Everything is uncovered and laid bare before the eyes of God, before the eyes of Him to whom we must give account. There is nothing that we do that is hidden from God. (Hebrews 4:13)

We who are in the Kingdom, should be different. Or, have we been captured by enemy, put in their outfits, and so we look just like them? Have we been captured by the world and sequestered away in *hidden*?

It is the glory of God to conceal a thing, but the honor of kings is to search it out, and you are the light of the world. You should be a city that's set upon a hill that cannot be hid, (Matthew 5:14).

So, we're asking the Lord to take us higher. From a higher vantage point, you can see so much more. If you're just standing on the street, looking across the street, you can see a few things. If you go up higher, say to a mountain, you can see all the way into the valleys. Amen.

When there is a storm coming, we need to seek safety. On an airplane, when storms occur, the pilot sometimes says we might be in the storm for a few minutes. Then the captain will take us to higher altitudes, so we'll be above the storm. In the same way, going higher in Christ, we can be above the storms of life. We can be seated in heavenly places in Christ Jesus. We could be hidden in Christ. We could be in the realm of Christ. We need spiritual eyes to see the storm and also to know how and where to go to be higher, in the Name of Jesus.

The name of the LORD is a strong tower:
the righteous runneth into it, and is safe.
(Proverbs 18:10)

So, in Christ we can survey the whole battlefield even in real time. Thank You, Lord. And once in Christ, we can shelter in place there until the battle or the wars are over.

Prayers

23. Lord, Jesus, forgive me of all my sins. Have your angels and camp around about me and my whole family, regarding this matter, and these prayers. Protect us and keep us safe against demonic attacks and retaliation of the devil and his demons, witchcraft or retaliation, in the Name of Jesus, Amen.

24. The *spirit of fear.* I bind that *spirit* that's causing people to be scared to see anything in the spirit, in the Name of Jesus.

25. Thank You, Lord. You make allowances for our weaknesses. You're patient and kind and loving towards us.

26. Lord, stop me from arguing with my flesh, and my guilty conscience, in the Name of Jesus.

27. Lord, let the love and Grace, Mercy, peace and righteousness of Jesus abound, in the Name of Jesus.

28. Thank You, Lord for helping me overcome. Deliver me from *fear*. You've given us love and power and a sound mind, and not *fear*, in the Name of Jesus.

29. Even if people don't believe what we know we see in the Spirit. Thank You, Lord for a sound mind, in Jesus' Name.

30. I cast down all evil imagination and every high thing that exalts itself against the knowledge of God.

31. I cast down every evil imagination. I cast down stuff I've watched on TV and movies, horror movies, horror stories told around campfires, in the Name of Jesus.

32. We are greater than all of that, in Jesus' Name.

33. Lord, forgive me for magnifying the devil at any time, for magnifying evil in any way. Lord, let us magnify You, in the Name of Jesus.

34. Father, You are the greatest power. You will never be defeated.

35. And even with feet for a high places, Lord, take me higher, let me soar like the eagle, in the Name of Jesus.

36. Let me hide in You far above all principalities and powers and spiritual wickedness in high places, in Jesus' Name.

37. Keep us safe from every storm, safe from any storm that may be coming, in the Name of Jesus.

38. Lord, give us spiritual eyes. Give me spiritual vision. Lord, open my eyes that I may see spiritually what's going on around me, in the Name of Jesus.

   • Lord arise; God arise and open my eyes, in the Name of Jesus.

39. Spiritual eyes open so that things are clear and that my dreams have proper meaning, in the Name of Jesus.

40. Lord, let me escape unnecessary hurt, harm, and failure, in the Name of Jesus.

41. Lord, let all lies of the enemy be exposed, and let me see Truth, in the Name of Jesus.

42. Let me see through the devil's masquerade, in Jesus' Name.

43. Lord, do not leave me out in the wilderness, bring me out of pits, out of dungeons, out of cages, out of prisons, out of every captivity, in the Name of Jesus.

44. Thank You, that I dwell in safety because of You, Lord, in the Name of Jesus.

45. Father, open my spiritual eyes, in the Name of Jesus, let me see what might be invisible even to others. Let me see what might not be cool to see.

46. Lord, let me see what might not be cool to my friends and family. Let me see what might even seem weird to them, if it's for Godly purpose, in the Name of Jesus.

47. Let me see so that I may pray for others. Let me see for those who don't want to see, or they can't see, or they won't pray for themselves in this season, in the Name of Jesus.

48. Lord, arise in the Thunder of Your power and defend Your interest in my life, in the Name of Jesus.

49. Power summoning anything, from the grave, be exposed, and die, in the Name of Jesus.
50. Every destruction assigned against me, catch Fire, in the Name of Jesus.
51. Any power pressing down my head, scatter, in the Name of Jesus.
52. Jesus, You are the lifter of my head.
53. Any power assigned to make me backslide, backfire, in the Name of Jesus.
54. Satanic conspiracy against my moving forward in life, scatter, in the Name of Jesus.
55. Strongmen in my family and my bloodline assigned to pull me down. Be bound and removed, in the Name of Jesus.
56. Gates against my progress and successes, be opened, now, in Jesus' Name.
57. Heaven over my prosperity heaven, over my career Heaven over my business and my family life, be opened by Fire, in the Name of Jesus.
58. Hidden weapons formed against my education, career, and prosperity, break! in the Name of Jesus.

59. Every arrow of fire against my head, backfire, in the Name of Jesus.
60. Powers saying that I won't succeed. I break you now, in Jesus' Name.
61. Every good thing stolen from me ever--, return to me and the entity that stole it, die by Fire, in the Name of Jesus.
62. I fire back every arrow of infirmity by the power in the Blood of Jesus.
63. Weapons formed against my health, die, in the Name of Jesus.
64. Hidden Weapons formed against my health, die, in the Name of Jesus. (X7)
65. Owners of evil load, hear the Word of the Lord today. Carry your own load, by Fire, in the Name of Jesus.
66. Demons assigned to turn my life upside down, die by Fire, in the Name of Jesus.
67. Holy Ghost, overshadow my whole life, in the Name of Jesus.
68. God arise, open the eyes of my understanding, in the Name of Jesus.
69. Father God, laugh all my opposition into derision and scorn by the power in the Blood of Jesus.

70. Chariots of Fire, horsemen of the Lord, overtake my enemies, in Jesus' Name. Every enemy that has marked me for destruction, receive double disgrace, in the Name of Jesus.

71. Every curse, come off my body and life by the power in the Blood of Jesus.

72. Hidden garments of shame, *reproach, failure, destruction, sickness, poverty* or *death,* catch Fire now and burn, burn, burn, in the Name of Jesus.

73. Burn to ashes, all evil clothing that you have for me, by Holy Ghost Fire, in the Name of Jesus.

74. I dump you into the dumpster and I set a Holy Ghost dumpster Fire, and bury you now, in the Name of Jesus.

75. I shall not be afraid. I shall not be afraid. I shall not be afraid. I shall not be afraid of sudden terror, pestilence, or any evil, day or night, in the Name of Jesus.

76. I cry for boldness, Lord, to confront every unknown, to confront every fear, every noise, every odd thing that appears to be happening to me, in me, or around me, in the Name of Jesus.

77. Lord, let me walk in purpose, Grace and anointing, that you've given me, to stamp out the works of the devil, so that nothing by any means will hurt me, in Jesus' Name.

78. Lord, shine Your light and give me Wisdom to know what to do in every situation, in the Name of Jesus.

79. Lord, grant me everything that I need; knowledge, Wisdom, anointing authority, confidence, boldness, and Holy Ghost power to deal with hidden sins and iniquity, in the Name of Jesus.

80. Holy Spirit deliver me, deliver me, Lord, in the Name of Jesus.

81. Lord, in my kingly and priestly anointing as a son of God, I ask You to show me all that I have not seen, all that I have not found, all that I have not discovered, all that I've been too fearful or too ignorant to see. Show me more. Show me, Father, in the Name of Jesus.

82. By the power of the Holy Spirit, let me become a different person, a better person, a stronger person in Christ who's not afraid, who does not doubt, who's

blessed to believe, even though I have not yet seen.

83. Give me the ability to deal with the things that You sent me here to Earth to deal with, in the Name of Jesus. Thank You, Lord.

84. I reject and destroy any point of contact with evil, especially any items related to *spirit spouse* in my house, workplace, or life, in the Name of Jesus.

85. I reject and reverse all defilement, in the Name of Jesus.

86. Lord cleanse me from all forced defilement; it is not my will to sin against You. Cleanse me, Lord, and I shall be whiter than snow, in the Name of Jesus.

87. Lord, cleanse me that I am not a sexual dumpster in the spirit, in the Name of Jesus.

88. Cleanse me Lord or every defilement; I repent; don't leave me outside the gate, in the Name of Jesus.

89. Lord, cleanse me, blot out every evil mark so that I don't attract witches, warlocks, and evil human astral projectors, in the Name of Jesus.

90. Lord, forgive me of every sin, whether there were hidden demonic transferences or not, in the Name of Jesus.
91. Lord, show me so I can repent, get rid of it, and be delivered fully delivered from all evil, in the Name of Jesus.
92. Eating and drinking in the dream, *spirit marriage*, sex in the dream, *spirit spouse, spirit children*, I reject it all, in the Name of Jesus. If I'm doing any of that or if it is happening to me, show me, Lord, so I can denounce it, in Jesus' Name.
93. I file for a divorce from *spirit spouse--*, every *spirt spouse* if there is more than one, in the Name of Jesus. I destroy all by Fire, in the Name of Jesus.
94. My life, receive Fire, become Fire, in the Name of Jesus. (X7 or more)
95. My life, my body, my health, my marriage, family, career, finances, especially *hidden spirit spouse*, come out, come out wherever you are and be bound and cast out, in the Name of Jesus.
96. Hidden *spirit spouse* or any *spirit spouse*, come out by Fire, and die, in the Name of Jesus.

97. And Lord, where I dreamed that my spouse was with another person, but You were showing me that my spouse has a *spirit spouse,* I ask for Wisdom and anointing to communicate it with my spouse so we can both pray together for the sake of covenant, marriage, and family success, all to Your glory. In the Name of Jesus. Amen.

98. Because there's nothing covered that shall not be revealed, neither is anything hidden that shall not be known, Lord, release me from the grips of every foul *spirit,* in the Name of Jesus.

99. Release me by Fire, in the Name of Yeshua.

100. Every *spirit spouse,* every *spirit wife, spirit husband,* die! I hate you with perfect hate, in the Name of Jesus.

101. Every evil foul thing that you've deposited into my life, come out by Fire, in the Name of Jesus.

102. *Spirit spouse,* any deposits I may have issued be burned up by Fire, in the Name of Jesus.

103. *Spirit spouse*, fall down and die, in the Name of Jesus.
104. I divorce from any marriage with *spirit spouse* or any evil, in the Name of Yeshua.
105. I am married to Christ, alone, in the Spirit, in the Name of Jesus.
106. I am married to my only Kingdom spouse, in the natural, in the Name of Jesus.
107. Lord, give us advance knowledge of the enemy's hidden plans against us, in the Name of Jesus.
108. Lord, give us advance knowledge of the storms that are upcoming, in the Name of Jesus.
109. Lord, give us how to pray against attacks from and for deliverance from any evil foundation, in the Name of Jesus.
110. Hidden ancestral curses: I break every evil ancestral covenant made with the evil one, in the Name of Jesus.
111. I break every curse that is a result of every evil covenant, in the Name of Jesus.

112. Every demon and devil entity sent to enforce any evil in my life, die, in the Name of Jesus.

113. Lord, let me escape unhurt and unharmed and like a mighty warrior completely defeat and destroy the enemy that is after me, in the Name of Jesus.

114. Lord, thank You for the victory and the spoils. Thank You, Lord for returning to me 7 times what they took from me.

115. You, evil devils, demons, and entities pay up, in the Name of Jesus.

116. And you're not taking anything else.

117. Jesus, hide me in Your secret place. And while I'm there, teach me, bring me up, bring me higher and higher to the Rock that is higher than I.

118. Teach me Your words, your ways, that I may not sin against you, in the Name of Jesus

119. .

120. In the whole armor of God, with Christ, as my Lord and Savior, He has made hope in glory. Amen.

121. Give me authority. I Accept the authority to speak to the storm and I decree, "Peace be still."

122. Give me Your peace, Lord, in my life my home, my workplace, my career, my marriage, my children, and my *children's* children to 1000 generations, in the Name of Jesus.

123. You be glorified. Lord, be glorified.

124. Lord, let hidden curses in my life be exposed and disgraced, in the Name of Jesus.

125. By the power in the Name of Jesus, I cancel every evil handwriting against me; I nail it to the Cross of Jesus.

126. I divorce *spirit spouse--*, every *spiritual spouse* forever, in the Name of Jesus.

127. Any hidden curse placed on me in the dream, by the power in the Blood of Jesus, I dismantle that curse and curse it to die, in the Name of Jesus.

128. Lord, reveal to me all my hidden sins, in the Name of Jesus.

129.   I break and *loose* my destiny from the destruction planned by hidden sins, hidden iniquity, and hidden curses, in the Name of Jesus.

130.   Heavenly Father, deliver me from all hidden sins, and hidden curses, in the Name of Jesus.

131.   Every disease, disorder, syndrome, illness or symptom because of hidden sin, hidden curses, night defilements, or *spirit spouse,* die with your curse, in the Name of Jesus.

132.   Hidden curses in my life, break and lose your power against me, in the Name of Jesus.

Hidden In Plain Sight

A person could be living under a curse or curses and not even know it. Not even realize it, because sometimes things are ignored, or they're explained away as just trivial things. *Everybody goes through this.* But things are not always just natural or trivial issues. Sometimes there are spiritual issues that need to be looked at with spiritual eyes. Spiritual problems need spiritual solutions, or else they will remain problems. Or they could get worse.

Deuteronomy 28 outlines curses that are right there for us to see. Are we looking? Are we seeing them with our spiritual eyes? So, I will mention a few things out of Deuteronomy 28.

Verses 1 through 14 are about the blessings that the Lord says will come upon us if we obey Him. Verses from 15 to 64 are about curses, and some of those verses have multiple curses within the same verse. So, there are a lot of curses. Therefore, we need to walk well, walk wisely, walk upright before the Lord, and we need to be wise. Amen.

Starting with some of the blessings, I want to challenge you, and the challenge is. I'm going to list some blessings. If these things have never happened to you, if you can say these things never have happened to you, **then you might be under a curse.**

The blessings of God should be pursuing you, overtaking you. The blessings of God should be looking for you. When you're in the right place, in the right position, and in the right condition, and at the right time, you should be blessed. But if you're not being blessed, then you might be under a curse. Defilement affects your placement, position, condition and timing; it can jump you into a corrupt and evil timeline.

Defilement, as in the Bible, puts you outside of the *gate* for at least a day, if you repent. If you do not repent you could be outside the presence of God for longer. If blessings are not pursuing you, you need to look deeper.

The Kingdom of Heaven is not neutral where nothing happens. Neither is Earth. All things that are alive are dynamic; things change day by day, hour by hour, moment by moment. But are those changes *seen* by us, or hidden from us?

Blessings of God are for the saved. OK, you can hear God, or at the very least, you know that God hears you and He answers your prayers. If that's never happened to you, you might be under a curse. Because we should be able to hear from God. We should be able to talk to God. We should be able to send prayers up to God and know that they're heard and answered.

The righteous cry, and the Lord heareth, and delivereth them out of all their troubles. (Psalm 34:17)

So, are you progressing in your education or your vocational endeavors?

That's happened to you. OK, good; your heavens, the heaven over you is open. As I said, your prayers are going up, and the blessings are coming down. OK. You're financially comfortable? Well off--, maybe even wealthy. Amen. Praise God. You are not weighed down with debt. Your credit cards are not maxed out. You don't have loans with every bank in town or even online. And if you have a mortgage, you have one mortgage (unless you are an investor) and not a second on your one mortgage? OK. I'd really like to be able to say you're totally debt free, now that's living under a blessing.

Owe no man anything but to love him. But to love one another for he that loveth another hath fulfilled the law. (Romans 13:8)

OK, so has this ever happened to you? You have savings; do you have at least one savings account? Amen. You're not stressed about money. You don't lose sleep thinking about bills or money or payments.

You love your house, you love your home you live in, you love where you live, and you have good neighbors. You have a retirement account. You've already at least started one.

You're not sick in your body. Good. Your marriage is fine, your children are blessed, and your children are a blessing to you; they're not a worry to you.

Wherever you go, people show you favor, or at least they don't disrespect you. Then you may be living under blessings. Amen.

If these things are not happening for you, then you might need to ask God. *Hey God, what's up?* It is not God that is the problem, so you may need to ask Him to show you hidden problems or hidden curses.

But you might say, *I do alright. Things aren't that bad in my life. I can't complain. I won't complain.*

Don't Get Used to Oppression

If you didn't know that your life is supposed to be better than it is, then get in the Word. If the enemy is oppressing you, have you gotten used to breadcrumbs--, the breadcrumbs that the devil is letting you have when you should have the whole loaf of bread? Even if you don't eat the whole loaf of bread. Because then you'd have enough to share. You'd have enough for Ministry, and you'd have enough to share with the poor and those less fortunate than you are.

So if that's the case, then maybe you should complain. Maybe you should complain about the devil, and maybe you should be complaining to your Father, God.

And that's called prayer. That's called warfare. Warfare, prayer.

Do not coexist with the devil. Do not try to coexist with the devil. Don't get comfortable with the devil. You get rid of the devil, You get the devil out of your life because the devil comes to steal, kill and destroy. You have to be adamant about this. The devil can't have what's yours, and he can't have what Jesus died for you to have. You can't just willingly give it up; fight.

If you bought your kid a new bike for his birthday, would you be OK if the bully down the block borrowed it for a few weeks? Would you be OK if the bully down the block wrecked it? Would you be OK if the bully down the block stole it and locked it up in his parents' garage?

No, you'd be livid. Well, God is sending you blessings, but God's not trying to bless the devil. So, we shouldn't be either.

If there were pests and roaches and ants in your house, would you feed them or would you try to get rid of them? Well, the devil is a pest. He doesn't belong in your life. He doesn't belong in your business. He doesn't belong in your finances. He doesn't belong in your body. He doesn't belong in your spiritual life, He doesn't belong in your future, your destiny, your ministry, your eternal destination. He doesn't belong anywhere around you. So, get some more of that holy indignation against the devil who's interfering in your life. Because if the devil's robbing you, he's also robbing your entire family, your children, your spouse, your well-being, your health, your ministry, your future, your legacy--, everything.

Your sin can impact everyone in your bloodline, even your siblings. It doesn't just open your spiritual doors, it could open family doors. You are your brother's keeper. If for no other reason than selfish reasons, you should care if your sibling is a sinner, or still a sinner. And, they should care if you're a sinner because this can affect the entire bloodline, and for generations to come. If you're going to snatch sinners from hell fire, start with the members of your own house.

Curses on Job

When we look at the curses that came upon job. The first thing that came upon him was a financial disaster, financial calamities. That's not happening to you, is it? But if it is, that's a sign that you could be living under a curse. The next thing that happened to Job was his children and his house. Everything was attacked. Job's children all died.

Are your children, OK? Is your house, your home, your marriage? Are they OK? If they're not, you could be under a curse.

I'm not just saying this just to irritate you or aggravate you or scare you. gonna give you the tools and the formulas that you need to live a prosperous, blessed life and to get out from under curses if you're under curses.

The next thing that happened to Job was he became sick in his body. Then after that, Job had friends that came over, but they weren't really respecting him or honoring him. They're pretty much telling him what's wrong with him. I don't know if those are friends, or not. I don't think they are.

That's not my definition of a friend. How about your friends? If you don't have friends, or at least one good friend, unless God has set you apart for a season, you could be under a curse.

These things are all serious clues that you might be under an evil spiritual oppression or curses. Are weird or bad things happening to you all the time? You may be on the edge of success, but then something crazy happens. Something unexpected, something unforeseen, something really impossible. But it happens to you, it keeps happening. You could be under a curse. I know too many people who jokingly expect the worst every day, all day.

And it's gotten so bad, you may not even want to make friends anymore, you may not even have hope anymore that you can even start something and finish it. And you don't even want to talk about your plans and your hopes anymore and your dreams. And maybe you actually shouldn't until you find out who you're telling it to. Only share with the right people. Pray and ask God,

But these odd things that keep happening to you--, it's so many odd things that people are beginning to think that you're making them up. But you're not. They really are happening to you.

I know, because I went through a phase in my life where the weirdest things happened to me, and I didn't know that I was possibly under a curse. That's why I'm sharing this message. So you'll know. And you'll know how to apply these questions to your life and how to look spiritually, and how to ask God about what's happening around you and in your life, so you can have the abundant life that Jesus came to Earth for you to have, and not be under a curse. And not be under. what the old folks call bad luck. You should not have to say, if it wasn't for bad luck, there'd be no luck at all.

Blessed Hands, Cursed Hands?

Instead, everything you set your hands to should be prospering; everything that you touch should be prospering,

But people who are under a curse what they touch with their hands, it'll either break, get corrupted, wither, and or die. They try to fix things, but they make it worse. They may try to build something, but they can't build it. They can't complete it, they can't finish it.

If you ever seen what I call a destructo-kid--, that's a kid who can tear up anything. They can break things that you didn't know could be broken. You need to pray for that kid if it's your kid, because you don't want them to grow up and stay like that.

Let's say they're 3, 4, or 5 years old now, when they get to be 15 their hands are still under a curse unless you do something. Pray! Pray now because my Bible says that everything I set my hands to do shall prosper.

133. O Lord, give me prospering hands now, in the Name of Jesus.

This is one of those times where we should complain. This is one of those times when we need to know the Word of God and know how to apply it to our lives, so we can know if we are under a curse or not.

We should not accept less than what the Word says, ever. We shouldn't accept mediocre, and we shouldn't give ourselves away and we should never give ourselves away to the devil.

I'm not saying everybody should be an engineer, architect or perfect craftsman, but things in your hands or near your hands should prosper and not fall apart. So, what can we do about it? We can pray, of course. Pray and resist the devil, and he will flee from you. (James 4:7)

Evaluate Your Life

As you apply the Word, look at your entire life very seriously. What's missing? What's wrong with it? Be truthful. If something is wrong in your life, is that because you are sinning? Then stop sinning; repent. Receive Jesus Christ as your Lord and Savior and repent even down your bloodline on both sides of your family. Go back 10 generations at least on each side, and then ask God to heal your family's foundation. Ask God to heal your family and to heal the problems in your bloodline. Ask Him to break any and all curses in your family line. Ask Him to bind the strongmen that are assigned against your life and against your family.

Ask God for restoration of all that's been lost or stolen from you. And then have faith and believe and receive the blessings that Jesus died for you to have.

It could be that you have a lucrative profession, you have a nice job, and you go there and things work out real well for you. Maybe you receive promotions, honors, respect, possibly even bonuses. Your work is appreciated and acknowledged; that's a blessing. That's living under the blessings, and that's what God intends.

But if the opposite is happening to you, you're frustrated at work, you're frustrated in your job, you're frustrated in your position, the boss is writing you up for something all the time. You're just not getting promoted or getting at least some increases in raises or bonuses or something, you could be under curs. You should be walking in a blessing and the blessings and possessions that should be pursuing you to overtake you. Anything different, anything less, we shouldn't pretend. Many times the reason why we don't possess our possessions is hidden right in plain sight.

If there's confusion in your family, in your house, in your world. brothers don't speak to brothers. sisters don't speak to sisters. Parents aren't speaking to this one or that one? It's because of a curse.

God is not the author of confusion. That's a curse. Or if you worry about sudden ruin or sudden ruin has already happened to you, that's a curse. If the enemies of God have you serving them, that's a curse. If you're a servant to people who should be your servants; that's a curse.

If you keep losing stuff, yeah, misplacing stuff, yeah, but also things being taken away from you, that is also loss. If that's happening, you're living under a curse. When you get things, but they just slip through your fingers, that's a curse. Maybe a house that bought or built--, a business or job, a car, a spouse, kids, savings account, or money. Don't risk losing your life, your legacy, your destiny by remaining under a hidden curse.

You feel oppressed. You feel like you're being ripped off and there's nobody to even help you. You work and work and work but where's the profit? You're watching other people prosper while you're not. All of that is a curse.

In Plain Sight

What may have been hidden from you may be right there in plain sight. If you've lost valuable property, other people now have what you've worked for, that's a curse. If you feel like curses follow you wherever you go, that might be a right feeling about the wrong things happening in your life. But if you are cursed or under a curse, then everywhere you go, there you are.

In the movies, people move from one city to the next, for a fresh start. But everywhere they go, there they are. I mean in cities and in states. There are territorial strongholds, curses, demons, principalities. But Deuteronomy 28 is talking about personal demons everywhere **you** go--. Going in, coming out, rising up, sitting down. In the field in the city. That's what the chapter says. That means cursed everywhere.

God gives us a way to get out from curses, in the Name of Jesus. So that dark cloud that's trying to follow you, and to rain on only you can be chased away permanently. The fact that there is trouble means there are curses and enforcing demons. The fact that there are curses means there are evil covenants. Evil covenants mean there are evil altars. All of this means there is iniquity, and it means sin happened and it was either not repented for or not forgiven.

You are not the guy who gets the speeding ticket on the way to work, and then you are late to work because you got the speeding ticket, are you? Then you get written up because you were late to work, and then you skip lunch because you have to make up time. At the end of your workday, you get to your car and you have a parking ticket. You're not that guy. When you get home, the utilities are shut off because you forgot to pay the bill.

No one should endure those kinds of problems, either in one day, one week, one month, one year. That is a curse. And that's where the curses are working in someone's life, that they're going through like that all the time, with weird stuff happening all the time. Unexplainable, impossible things happening all the time.

Stuff happens, and some of the stuff that happens is spiritual. We may be overlooking it, or ignoring it, or pretending it didn't just happen. Maybe we're embarrassed to tell anybody. Folks, we cannot coexist with the devil; there is no place for him in our Godly lives.

If he or his demons have imposed themselves into your life, we'll only see frustrations, and losses, and disappointment. If we don't complain to God about it, if we don't pray about it. If we don't go into warfare about it, it's gonna multiply. It's gonna build up, and get worse. And that means we haven't resisted the devil then he's just gonna bring more and more of is evil friends, until a person is finally overwhelmed.

If he has his way, he won't be satisfied until his victim is overtaken and destroyed. There is no room for him in our lives.

But when the curse is right in front of you, complain. Complain to God. When the curse is hidden but the effects of the curse are not—complain to God. Report to Heaven; complain in prayer, in spiritual warfare; complain in the Courts of Heaven.

If you didn't know it was a curse but thought it was *just life*, get in the Word and find out what your life should be like. People who live with curses--, you may hear them say, *Ohh, that's just life.* Folks, it the life the devil planned for you; **God did not plan a horrible life for you.**

Maybe this is life for the unsaved, but we're not the unsaved. It is not life for us. It is not life for the people, of God. Jesus came that we may have life and have it more abundantly.

Read the Signs

God shows us signs and wonders, and sometimes the signs are in our dreams. But we ignore them. Please don't ignore your dreams. We may not know what dreams mean. They may seem silly or ridiculous, like they don't even apply to us. Sometimes we may think they're not even important, but they are.

Or sometimes we have a dream that we tell to the wrong people. Maybe tell it to somebody who is not even a Christian or somebody who doesn't have a clue about dreams, symbols, interpretations, and what things mean spiritually We got to tell it to the right person.

There are some dreams, even good ones that you tell to NO ONE. Joseph could have avoided a lot of trouble if he had kept his mouth shut.

There are many keys to a successful life for us, right in plain sight, in our dreams. But they're hidden if we lack knowledge to understand them or know what we need to do to understand those dreams that we have in the night.

So, what do we do? What do we need to do? Here's the answer. You ready? Remember your dreams. If you don't remember your dreams, pray to remember your dreams. Ask God via the Holy Spirit to help you remember your dreams. Record your dreams and then you get Christ centered interpretation from your dreams or of your dreams. And then you pray about your dreams. Evil dreams need to be cancelled right away.

Holy Spirit inspired dreams are from God and should be accepted and celebrated. You still pray and we have to be wise. God is trying to show us something. The only reason that your dreams will be missing, covered, hidden, or cloaked is because something happened in the dream that the devil tricked you or did something in your dream life. That opens the door for him to come into your life in the natural and do something diabolical to you. He wants you to not know what he did. That's why you have to pray.

If you don't know what you dreamed, cancel the dream. Cancel whatever happened at night while you were asleep, in detail, cancel it, in the Name of Jesus. Any evil dream, if you think it's an evil dream, if you know it's an evil dream, cancel it right away. Because if you let the devil in, he's gonna add more and more problems to your life until you are overwhelmed or destroyed.

The first curse that he can get into your world gives him license to come in and operate in your life. A curse can last many generations in the family line. It can last as long in a bloodline until somebody in that bloodline, somebody saved and aware breaks the curse over their family. And is that you?

For some reason, I believe it's you.

Grievous Oppression

Deuteronomy 28:52-53 says you will be unsuccessful in everything you do. Day after day you will be oppressed and robbed with no one to rescue you. Because of the suffering your enemy will inflict on you during your siege, you will eat the fruit of the womb, the flesh of the sons and daughters the Lord your God has given you. And I'm not going to describe that in a literal sense. I'm not sure exactly how God meant it. He could have meant it literally or figuratively.

I've seen people who are so financially strapped, so financially oppressed by the devil. The financial curse that they're living under is so heavy, that what they have to do is just to try to survive is mind boggling.

I've seen people so oppressed and they're living ahead of their own life, or maybe they're so behind in their own life that they've just sucked up their kids' lives. They're using their kids' names and Social Security numbers to set up accounts to buy things. They're just waiting for their kids to finish school so the kids can take care of the parents. Maybe they're waiting for the kids to finish school so the kids can be the parents' retirement.

These are all curses.

Cannibalism was spoken of in the Book of Deuteronomy. If you're willing to sacrifice your child and your child's future, there's something wrong with that. If a person is willing to sacrifice their child's future, even to the point of pretending there's something wrong with the child in order to get government benefits--, that's cannibalism. This is a curse. This is putting your child under a curse. And this is you also living under a curse in getting over. It is a curse. It is not a blessing. It is not neutral. It is not nothing. It is a curse.

So now the devil's got the parents and the children. You think it's time to pray yet? Do you think it's time to take action yet? Do you think it's time to get saved and to learn about spiritual warfare yet? I do.

Here's another curse. You live in constant suspense. I call that survival mode. And you're filled with dread night and day, never sure about your life, never sure about what's gonna happen, just waiting for the other shoe to drop --, that's a curse. No peace is a curse.

Families breaking up is a curse. Children are lost from a family? These are all mentioned in the Bible and that's a curse.

When you serve your servants, that's a curse.

Are there giants in your bloodline that your ancestors didn't fight and conquer? Someone in your bloodline will have to fight them. Is it you? I think it is you. You're gonna have to fight those giants, those spiritual giants, and you're going to have to be victorious in order to have a victorious life over them.

If you're under a curse, you're really serving the devil. He wants you broken, busted, and sick, living a lackluster life.

Jesus came to redeem us from sickness, from poverty, from the curse of the law, and from eternal damnation. We should be living a life free of these frustrations, and emotional pain and physical pain. Because all of that is hell, it is a form of hell.

Jesus came for us to not have to be in hell or live that way. You know, the most stubborn curses are the hidden ones. They're the hidden curses, and they are the most wicked. And they're most often the most often used weapon of the devil. He likes to hide. The devil needs to be stopped in his tracks against your family.

I think it's you who will be the battleaxe. You're the one in your family who needs to break these curses in your bloodline. Glory to God.

Prayer & Wisdom

A curse is a spiritual problem that can only be solved spiritually. Two keys right here will help you solve these spiritual type problems. One is prayer. and the other is Wisdom.

In Hosea 4:6 God says that His people are destroyed for lack of knowledge. You need to learn all you can about curses. Recall that where sin remains, curses also remain. Stop sinning, repent, repent for everybody under your authority, and even repent for your ancestors. Every curse brings at least one demon to enforce it and to torment your life. The magnitude of the curse determines the strength of the demon that comes with it, or the quantity of demons that come with the curse, or curses.

When a blessing is released, angels of God are also released. But when there's a curse, demons are released.

Someone could issue a curse without a reason. There are people who dabble in the dark arts, but if someone tries to send a curse to you and they can't because there's nothing in you, there's no sin in you, it won't land. Like Jesus said, *The prince of this world has nothing in Me,* likewise let there be nothing of the devil in you. So, if somebody tries to send a curse to you and there's no way for it to a light on you, it will go back to the person who sent it.

But that curse can also go back, because once they are found out and you do your prayer work, you can do return to sender prayers and send them back, in Jesus' Name.

Hidden curses can come in a number of ways.

- Broken marriage vows and covenants.

Be careful here. God hates broken covenants. If God put a marriage together, I personally don't believe it can be broken. But, if you're in a marriage or have been married and you know good and well, God didn't put it together—that it was all flesh that put it together, then it can easily be broken.

Talk to God about this.

Here's another way that curses can come:

- Any ungodly sexual covenant. Covenants are sealed with sex, so I'm talking about ungodly illegal sex.

You may have been in relationships, and been in sexual situations with people, but you need to break the covenant that you made through the sex that you had with that person, no matter how long ago it's been. No matter how long it's been since you saw that person. If not, that covenant you made can hinder or stop good things and progress in your life. It can bring on curses. Especially if the other person is bitter or still bitter about you, then your life will also be bitter and that is a curse. You've forgotten all about it. You forgot the sex, the person, even the whole act, but it formed an evil covenant. The evil covenant promotes a curse. The curse sends in at least one demon to enforce it. Demons oppress. Demons can also hide. The curse is hidden to you, but your life is frustrated. There's your answer.

Repent.

Doing wrong to people in business can bring a curse. Getting wealth unrighteously also brings curses into a person's life. False acquisition of properties can bring curses. Never claim property that is not your own and that you know you're not supposed to claim. Don't buy stolen items.

A cursed person will labor in their work with little to no profit to show for it. Ancestral, parental, familial, and foundational curses are famous for hidden iniquity.

- Touching anything unclean or anything related to an idol can bring curses into a person's life. And then there are curses from premarital sex.

How To Pray Against Hidden Curses

Praying against a curse that you don't have doesn't hurt you, it doesn't hurt anything, but not praying against the curse that you do have, hurts everything.

Deal with the power behind the curse. Pray prevailing prayers. A two-sentence prayer is not enough--, something like, *Oh Jesus, fix it.* No, it takes way more than that. You've got to engage your spirit and soul and put your whole being into your prayers.

You have to pray every day for more than an hour, 2 hours or more a day, for weeks, for days, for weeks, for months, even longer. **FYI: A prayer watch is 3 hours.**

The Holy Spirit will give you release when you've prayed enough. You may also feel or discern that the curse has been lifted and the demons have left you.

How long and how often do you pray? It depends on how bad the oppression is in your life, how bad the curse is; however, there is no set formula. It depends on how embedded the hidden curse is in your bloodline, how destructive this curse is, how dangerous it is. How crucial it is for you break it, and how passionate you are about breaking it as to what kind of energy and passion you're gonna put into learning about it and actually praying. You need to hate every demon with perfect hate.

Remember, the devils like to hide and pretend they're not there. You've got to be relentless going after them until they're gone, until your life becomes what the true Lord Jesus intended it to be.

Prayer Points

And Jesus said that when you stand praying, ask for forgiveness. So that should be the first thing you do. Ask God for forgiveness.

134. Father, forgive me for every sin against You. If I'm under divine judgment, Father, I pray Mercy. I ask You to release me from any divine curse that by my own disobedience, rebellion, and sin I have bought onto myself, in Jesus' Name.

135. Lord, I forgive myself, in the Name of Jesus.

136. Father, I forgive all those who have offended me, and I release all unforgiveness, all bitterness and fear, because fear has torment.

137.   Lord, I break every evil covenant in my family line back 10 generations on both sides, by the Blood of Jesus.

138.   And by the blood of Jesus. I dismantle every curse and reverse every evil effect, in the Name of Jesus,

139.   I break every evil covenant I have made knowingly or unknowingly, in the dream, in my sleep, in the Name of Jesus.

140.   Father, every evil covenant holding me down that says I will not go, or I will not progress--, break now, in the Name of Jesus.

141.   Father, please bring full deliverance now, in the Name of Jesus.

142.   Father, I beg Mercy, in the name of Jesus and I send back every evil arrow that has been fired at me since my birth.

143.   In the Name of Jesus, I send back every evil arrow fired at the foundation of my life.

144.   In the Name of Jesus, I fire back every evil arrow fired of the foundation of my bloodline and my family line.

145.   In the Name of Jesus, in the whole armor of God, the helmet of salvation, the

breastplate of righteousness, the shield of faith, the sword of the Spirit, the belt of truth. My feet are shod with the Gospel of the preparation of peace and the cloak of Zeal, I enter into prayer, warfare prayer, declaring enemies of God. You have found out and you must leave. now, in the Name of Jesus. Go to the place of the true Lord Jesus has prepared for you, for early torment.

146. Your sentence is for failed assignment. Get out of my life. The Blood of Jesus is against you.

147. I break every curse associated with every evil covenant, in the Name of Jesus.

148. I break the curse of cursed hands.

149. I break the curse of cursed feet.

150. I break the curse of cursed legs.

151. I break the curse of cursed mind or brain.

152. I break the curse of failure at the point of almost there.

153. I break the curse of mistakes, errors, and making bad decisions and bad choices, in Jesus' Name.

154. I break every barrier of my life. Every barrier that is put up before me, every locked door, every padlock. I break them, in the Name of Jesus.

155. I break every chain and padlock off my life, in Jesus' Name.

156. I break every rope and shackle off my feet and off my life, in Jesus' Name.

157. I bind every strongman and every demon in place to enforce the curse, whether I know what the curse is or not, in the Name of Jesus.

158. I bind the *spirit of error*. I bind the *spirit of lust* and all sexual sins, in Jesus' Name.

159. I bind the *spirits of laziness, procrastination, stubbornness, rebellion, and disobedience*. I bind *dishonesty* and cheating, in Jesus' Name.

160. Lord, in every interpersonal relationship, I bind the *spirits of lying, cheating, stealing,* and taking what is not mine.

161. I bind *shame*, in the Name of Jesus, I bind the *spirit of failure* in the Name of Jesus.

162. I bind every other *spirit* that is working against me in this matter, in the Name of Jesus.

163. I bind idolatry, and I *loose* the love of God, the Spirit to worship and to serve only God.

164. I bind all evil, *lust, perversion*, and *greed*. I *loose* purity in the Holy Spirit.

165. I bind all works of the flesh. I *loose* all the Fruits of the Spirit, in the Name of Jesus.

166. I cast out every demon behind the curse and every demon sent to enforce the curse in Jesus' Name.

167. I claim the blessings of God for my life, in the Name of Jesus.

168. I command the devil to stop in his tracks right now, and get behind me, in Jesus' Name.

169. I possess my possessions and everything that belongs to me in my life, my family, my ministry, my business, in the Name of Jesus.

170. Lord, restore to me everything the enemy has stolen from me sevenfold. You have been found out devil; pay up!

171. Lord, redeem the time, in Jesus' Name. Lord, restore the years, in Jesus' Name.

172. Lord, heal the hurts and bind up every wound and every broken heart that has resulted from this curse or these curses, in Jesus' Name.

173. Bless me. Bless me, indeed. I am blessed that everything I set my hands to prospers.

174. I am blessed going in and coming out. I'm above only and not beneath. I am the righteousness of God in Christ Jesus.

175. I have abundance; there is no lack, in the Name of Jesus.

176. I enjoy the Peace of God. I enjoy His Shalom. There is nothing missing, nothing broken.

177. I live in peace, and I dwell in safety. I enjoy my home, my neighbors, and my neighborhood in safety and in peace, in Jesus' Name.

178. I am debt free, in the Name of Jesus.

179. There is no lack, there is no insufficiency. I have abundance; there's more than enough.

180. Promotion comes from the Lord.

181. Lord, surprise me with overdue promotion and good success.

182. I am blessed every day, every morning, every night, and the wealth of the wicked is laid up for the just.

183. I am justified in Christ Jesus. I declare.

184. I declare the positive word and the words of God. His praise will continually be in my mouth, my life. My mouth is full of blessings, so much that there's not room enough to contain it all.

185. The Lord has opened up the windows of Heaven. My heaven is open above me.

186. He's opened up the doors and the floodgates, and He is pouring out blessings on me that there's not room enough to receive, in the Name of Jesus.

187. I am blessed with blessings that are running over, in the Name of Jesus.

188. I have more than enough to share, and no devil can separate me from the love of God that is in Christ Jesus.

189. And no devil will separate me from the blessings that Jesus died that I may

enjoy on this Earth right now, in Jesus' Name.

190. And Lord, release the angels of blessings to locate and bless me now, in Jesus Name.

191. Angels of opportunity locate me now and lead me to opportunities and lead opportunities to me, in Jesus' Name.

192. Angels of healing, you're loosed to bring healing to every part of my life, my body, every organ, every cell, every muscle, every joint, every system, in the Name of Jesus.

193. Restore me Lord, to better than perfect health, as You intended from the beginning, in Jesus Name.

194. Father, I give thanks to You, and I thank You, and I bless You for setting me free and for blessing me mightily.

195. Father, You be magnified, be glorified, and let my blessed life be an example for many to see, to be drawn to You, Father, in Jesus' Name, Amen. Amen.

196. I seal these decrees and declarations across every dimension, era, age, realm

and timeline, past, present, and future. I seal them with the Blood of Jesus and the Holy Spirit of Promise, in the Name of Jesus.

197.   Any retaliation against this author, the reader, or anyone who will pray these prayers at any time in the future, backfire on the perpetrator, without Mercy and to infinity, in the Name of Jesus.

AMEN

Dear Reader

Thank you for acquiring and reading this book. I pray it inspires you to look deeply and always ask the Lord to sharpen your spiritual vision.

Shalom,

Dr. Marlene Miles

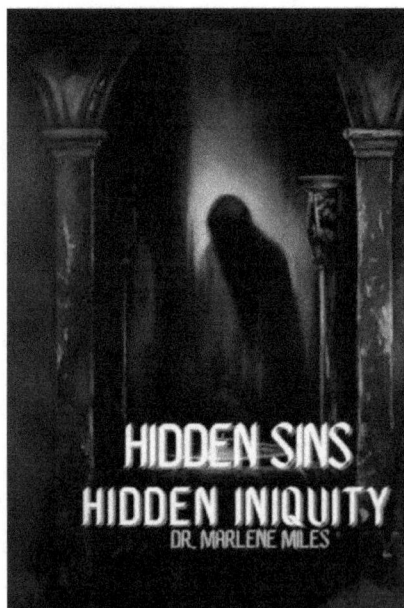

HIDDEN SINS
HIDDEN INIQUITY
DR. MARLENE MILES

Prayerbooks by this author

While most books by this author have prayer points either throughout the book or at the end, there are some books that are only prayers. You just open up the book and pray. They are listed below:

Prayers Against Barrenness: *For Success in Business and Life*

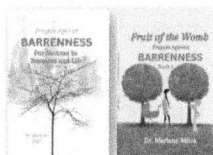

Fruit of the Womb: *Prayers Against Barrenness*

Beauty Curses, *Warfare Prayers Against*
https://a.co/d/5Xlc20M

Courts of Marriage: Prayers for Marriage in the Courts of Heaven *(prayerbook)*
https://a.co/d/cNAdgAq

Courtroom Warfare @ Midnight
(prayerbook) https://a.co/d/5fc7Qdp

Demonic Cobwebs *(prayerbook)*
https://a.co/d/fp9Oa2H

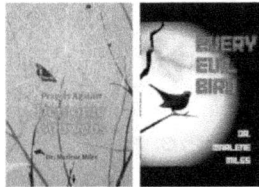

Every Evil Bird https://a.co/d/hF1kh1O

Gates of Thanksgiving

Spirits of Death, Hell & the Grave, Pass Over Me and My House

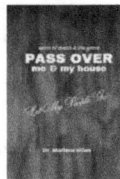

Throne of Grace: Courtroom Prayer

Warfare Prayer Against Poverty
https://a.co/d/bZ61lYu

Other books by this author

AK: The Adventures of the Agape Kid

Already Married in the Spirit: *Why You May Not Be Married in the Natural*

AMONG SOME THIEVES

Ancestral Powers

Anti-Marriage, *The Spirit of*

Backstabbers https://a.co/d/gi8iBxf

Barrenness, *Prayers Against* https://a.co/d/feUltIs

Battlefield of Marriage, *The*

Beware of the Dog: Prayers Against Dogs in the Dream.

Bless Your Food: *Let the Dining Table be Undefiled*

Blindsided: *Has the Old Man Bewitched You?* https://a.co/d/5O2fLLR

Break Free from Collective Captivity

Broken Spirits & Dry Bones

Casting Down Imaginations

Churchzilla, The Wanna-Be, Supposed-to-be Bride of Christ

Demonic Cobwebs (prayerbook)

Demonic Time Bombs

Demons Hate Questions

Devil Loves Trauma, *The*

Devil Weapons: Unforgiveness, Bitterness,...

The Devourers: Thieves of Darkness 2

Do Not Swear by the Moon

Don't Refuse Me, Lord (4 book series)
https://a.co/d/idP34LG

Dream Defilement

The Emptiers: *Thieves of Darkness, 1*
https://a.co/d/5I4n5mc

Evil Touch

Failed Assignment

Fantasy Spirit Spouse
https://a.co/d/hW7oYbX

FAT Demons (The): *Breaking Demonic Curses* https://a.co/d/4kP8wV1

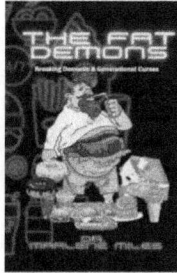

The Fold (5-book series)

- The Fold (Book 1)
- Name Your Seed (Book 2)
- The Poor Attitudes of Money (3)
- Do Not Orphan Your Seed (4)
- For the Sake of the Gospel (5)
- My Sowing Journal

Gang Ups: Touch Not God's Anointed

Getting Rid of Evil Spiritual Food

https://a.co/d/i2L3WYQ

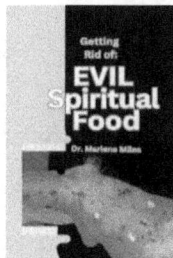

got HEALING? Verses for Life

got LOVE? Verses for Life

got HOPE? Verses for Life

got money? https://a.co/d/g2av41N

Here Come the Horns: *Skilled to Destroy* https://a.co/d/cZiNnkP

Hidden Sins: Hidden Iniquity

How to Dental Assist

How to Dental Assist2: Be Productive, Not Wasteful

How to STOP Being a Blind Witch or Warlock

I Take It Back

Legacy

Let Me Have A Dollar's Worth https://a.co/d/h8F8XgE

Level the Playing Field

Living for the NOW of God

Lose My Location https://a.co/d/crD6mV9

Love Breaks Your Heart

Made Perfect In Love

Man Safari, *The*

Marriage Ed. Rules of Engagement & Marriage

Made Perfect in Love

Money Hunters: Beware of Those

Money on the Altar https://a.co/d/4EqJ2Nr

Mulberry Tree, *The* https://a.co/d/9nR9rRb

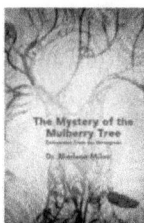

Motherboard (The) - *Soul Prosperity Series*

Name Your Seed

Occupy: *Until I Return*

Plantation Souls

Players Gonna Play

Power Money: Nine Times the Tithe

https://a.co/d/gRt41gy

The Power of Wealth *(forthcoming)*

Powers Above

The Robe, Part 1, The Lessons of Joseph

The Robe, Part II, The Lessons of Joseph

Seasons of Grief

Seasons of Waiting

Seasons of War

Second Marriage, Third--, *Any Marriage*

https://a.co/d/6m6GN4N

Sift You Like Wheat

Six Men Short: What Has Happened to all
the Men?

Soul Prosperity soul prosperity series 3

https://a.co/d/5p8YvCN

Souls Captivity soul prosperity series 2

The Spirit of Anti-Marriage

The Spirit of Poverty

StarStruck

SUNBLOCK

The Swallowers: *Thieves of Darkness*, 3

Take It Back

This Is NOT That: How to Keep Demons
from Coming at You

Time Is of the Essence

Too Many Wives: *Why You Have Lady Problems*

Tormenting Spirits
https://a.co/d/dAogEJf

Toxic Souls

Triangular Power *(series)*

- Powers Above
- SUNBLOCK
- Do Not Swear by the Moon
- STARSTRUCK

Unbreak My Heart: *Don't Let Me Die*

Uncontested Doom

Unguarded Hours, *The*

Unseen Life, *The* (forthcoming)

Upgrade: How to Get Out of Survival Mode

- Toxic Souls (Book 2 of series)
- Legacy (Book 3 of series)

The Wasters: *Thieves of Darkness,* Bk 2
https://a.co/d/bUvI9Jo

What Have You to Declare? What Do You Have With You from Where You've Been?

When I Was A Child, *I Prayed As a Child*

When the Devourer is Rebuked

https://a.co/d/1HVv8oq

The Wilderness Romance *(series)* This series is about conducting a Godly relationship and marriage with someone who is a Wilderness person. It is about how to recognize it and navigate through it. These books are about how not to get caught up in such.

- *The Social Wilderness*
- *The Sexual Wilderness*
- *The Spiritual Wilderness*

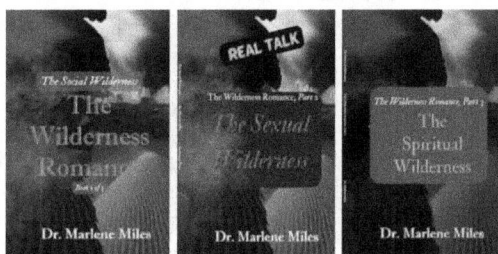

Other Series

The Fold (a series on Godly finances)
https://a.co/d/4hz3unj

Soul Prosperity Series https://a.co/d/bz2M42q

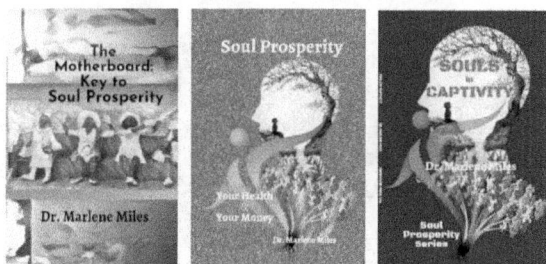

Spirit Spouse books

https://a.co/d/9VehDSo

https://a.co/d/97sKOwm

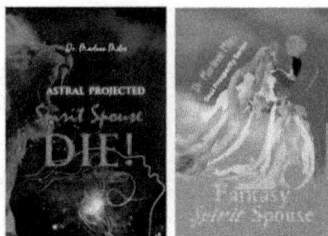

Battlefield of Marriage, The

https://a.co/d/eUDzizO

Players Gonna Play

https://a.co/d/2hzGw3N

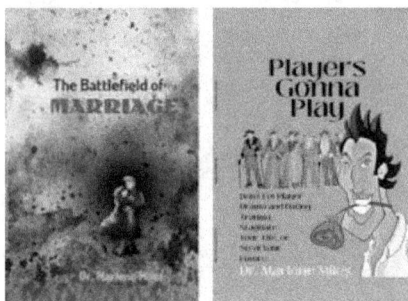

Matters of the Heart

Made Perfect in Love
https://a.co/d/7OMQW3O

Love Breaks Your Heart
https://a.co/d/4KvuQLZ

Unbreak My Heart https://a.co/d/84ceZ6M

Broken Spirits & Dry Bones
https://a.co/d/e6iedNP

Thieves of Darkness series

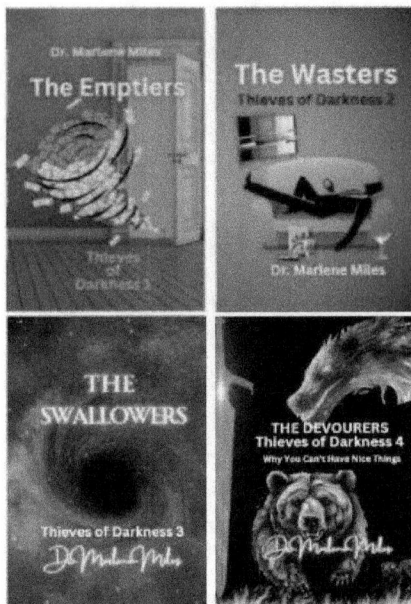

The Emptiers https://a.co/d/heio0dO

The Wasters https://a.co/d/5TG1iNQ

The Swallowers https://a.co/d/1jWhM6G

The Devourers: Why We Can't Have Nice Things
https://a.co/d/87Tejbf

Triangular Powers https://a.co/d/aUCjAWC

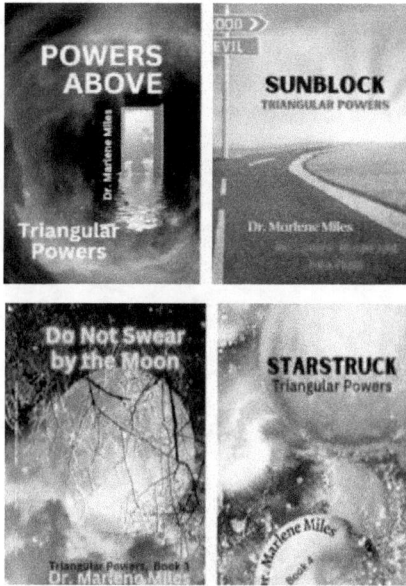

Upgrade (series) *How to Get Out of Survival Mode* https://a.co/d/aTERhX0